We never forget our own special Christmas memories, the toys we were desperate to have and the games we used to play. The classic TV shows and the festive number ones. It all sums up The Great British Christmas.

From the seasonal card to the fir tree and the turkey dinner, many of the traditions we enjoy today have their roots in the Victorian era, where our journey begins.

It is difficult to imagine now but there was a time when Christmas was hardly celebrated and, at the beginning of the 19th century, many businesses did not even consider it a holiday.

But the Victorians helped transform the occasion into what it is today, spreading the season of goodwill and making it a celebration for the whole family to enjoy.

Daily Mirror photographers have been there to record our festive celebrations for well over a century – and this magazine is packed with amazing images from the archive.

From the wartime truce of 1914 to the volunteers who took on the task of lifting festive spirits during the Second World War, Christmas brings out the best in people even in the toughest of times, and these stories are recounted here.

The rise of television added to the festive magic, as families sat together to watch the legendary Morecambe and Wise specials and the premieres of Hollywood blockbusters, while the Christmas number one single became a pop culture phenomenon.

The celebrations have become ever more extravagant but we take a look back on the fun we had before computer games were invented and provide recipes for traditional festive fare to give you another taste of Yuletide in the good old days.

Christmas is the most special time of the year and, in this magazine, you will be reminded just why.

Heritage Editor: Harri Aston
Designer: Ben Renshaw
Additional picture research: Lisa Thomson

With special thanks to Professor Mark Connelly, author of Christmas: A History

Part of the Mirror Collection
© 2013 Trinity Mirror. All Rights Reserved

Managing Director: Ken Rogers
Publishing Director: Steve Hanrahan
Executive Art Editor: Rick Cooke
Senior Editor: Paul Dove
Senior Marketing Executive: Claire Brown
Photosales: 0845 300 3021
Images: Mirrorpix, PA Photos
Printed by: PCP

A FESTIVE REBIRTH

HOW THE VICTORIANS HELPED TO CREATE A CRACKING CHRISTMAS

From Christmas trees and crackers to carol singing and the turkey dinner, the Victorians helped transform the festive period into what it is today, spreading the theme of goodwill and making it a celebration for the whole family to enjoy.

Main picture: Children learning about the Victorian Christmas at Osborne House in the Isle of Wight. Image courtesy of English Heritage

We actually have a German to thank for introducing some of the most prominent aspects of the British Christmas to these shores.

Queen Victoria's husband, Prince Albert, helped to make the Christmas tree as popular in Britain as they already were in his native country when he brought one to Windsor Castle in the 1840s.

The Illustrated London News published a drawing of the royal family celebrating around a decorated Christmas tree in 1848. Soon, virtually every home in Britain had a tree adorned with candles, sweets, fruit, homemade decorations and small gifts. The first Christmas cards were introduced in 1843 by Sir Henry Cole, who had asked his friend, artist John Calcott Horsley, to design a holiday card that would replace his seasonal task of writing many letters. ⊘

Above left: A drawing of the royal family celebrating around a decorated Christmas tree in 1848

Above right: Charles Dickens reading extracts from A Christmas Carol

Right: The first Christmas card, created in 1843

"SOON, VIRTUALLY EVERY HOME IN BRITAIN HAD A TREE ADORNED WITH CANDLES, SWEETS, FRUIT, HOMEMADE DECORATIONS AND SMALL GIFTS "

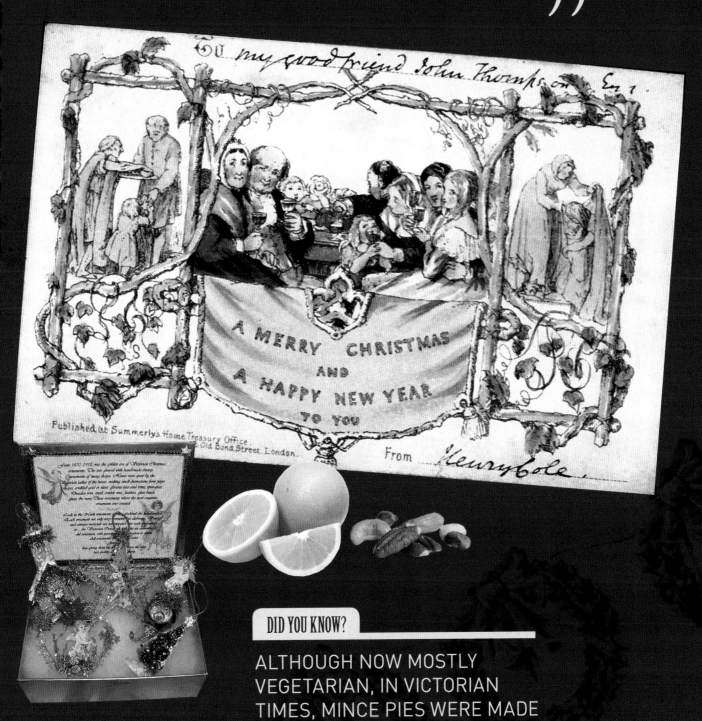

SMITH CAME UP WITH THE IDEA OF A SIMPLE PACKAGE WHICH SNAPPED WHEN PULLED APART

Above: Factory workers putting together Christmas crackers in 1955

Left: Victorian Christmas decorations at Osborne House in the Isle of Wight. Image courtesy of English Heritage

⊘ Shortly afterwards, London sweet-maker Tom Smith invented the Christmas cracker. After spotting French bonbons wrapped in paper with a twist at each end in 1847, he came up with the idea of a simple package filled with sweets that snapped when pulled apart. The sweets were replaced by small gifts and paper hats, and remain an essential part of modern Christmas. ⊘

At the start of Victoria's reign, children's toys tended to be handmade and expensive but games, dolls and books gradually became more affordable as mass production took off. However, a child from a poor family could still only expect to receive an apple, orange and a few nuts in their Christmas stocking, which became popular from around 1870.

Victorians also helped to revive the tradition of carol singing, introduced turkey as the centrepiece of the Christmas dinner and transformed the idea of the occasion so that it became centred around the family.

Charles Dickens' book A Christmas Carol – with its themes of family, charity, goodwill, peace and happiness – is also credited with helping to popularise and spread the traditions of the festival.

Above left: In this illustration, a maid sits knitting while a small boy places his letter to Father Christmas. His older sister looks on as she writes hers

Right: Rehearsals for a musical version of A Christmas Carol in 1958

DID YOU KNOW?

MANY THEOLOGIANS BELIEVE THAT JESUS WASN'T BORN ON DECEMBER 25 BUT SOMETIME IN SEPTEMBER BETWEEN 6BC AND 30AD.

1900-1919

PLENTY OF FUN AND GAMES IN THE DAYS BEFORE TELEVISION

With supermarkets still a long way off, a busy shopping trip was needed to bring Christmas dinner to the table, while a football match on the Western Front came to epitomise the season of goodwill.

Main picture: British soldiers wearing Christmas hats in a trench in France during the First World War. Top left, British and German troops photographed together during the Christmas truce

CHILDREN growing up in Edwardian Britain rarely received more than one present at Christmas.

For boys, toy soldiers were very popular and, for girls, dolls and tea sets, although the teddy bear was also gaining tremendous popularity at the time.

Pens, stationery sets and grooming kits would be given to adults, while more affluent families could afford gramophones.

The big day itself would start with a visit to the church, with the tree having been brought into the house and decorated the night before.

Although many items would have been bought in department stores, which had emerged in the late 1860s, there was no trip to the supermarket for festive food in Edwardian times. Instead, women had to visit several shops – butchers, spice merchants, bakers and grocers. ⊙

Above: Entertainer Gus Elen distributes toys to children in London in 1910

Right: Street hawkers in London at Christmas in 1912

ADVICE TO HOUSEWIVES FOR CHRISTMAS

Special Recipes for Use with Sandow's Wonderful New Baking Powder.

HOW YOU MAY MAKE ALL YOUR PUDDINGS, CAKES, AND PASTRIES DOUBLY DELIGHTFUL AND SPLENDIDLY NUTRITIOUS AND WITH GREATER ECONOMY

THE introduction of Mr. Sandow's wonderful new Baking Compound at this Festive Season, when the thoughts of pudding, cake and pastry-making are exercising the minds of every housewife, has proved a wonderful culinary aid. The cook finds that half the trouble of her pastry-making is overcome, and she is delighted with the every-time-splendid results achieved. She can hardly believe her eyes when she sees cakes or pastries coming from the oven far bigger in size than she anticipated, and then when cut there is a splendid evenness of texture and a lightness and crispness that denote complete success.

How delicious mother, father and the little ones find the new cakes, pastries or puddings in which Sandow's Baking Powder has been used! How eager the children are for more! And mother may well let them have it, for every particle of cake, pastry, pudding, etc., made with Sandow's Baking Powder is not only pleasing to the palate but splendidly nutritious.

Mr. Sandow is desirous that no home should be without this good Christmas Cheer, and he has given here five ideal recipes which will solve many a housewife's difficulty and provide every family with puddings, cakes, and pastries that every one will enjoy for the happy Christmas days.

Even if the housewife prefers to use her own recipes, she will find that by incorporating Sandow's Baking Powder, the results of her cooking will be a hundred-fold better in every way than they were before.

Here are the five recipes, and if you want double pleasure from your Christmas pudding; if you want every visitor a delighted guest, and every member of your family happy and contented, use the ingredients given in these recipes, being sure that you have SANDOW'S BAKING POWDER and no other. Sandow's Baking Powder ensures Economy, Nourishment and Digestibility and Saves Time and Labour.

Excellent Plain Biscuits.—Roll out a portion of bread dough made with Sandow's Baking Powder, and sprinkle with tiny pieces of butter; knead in well, roll to a quarter of an inch thick, prick well all over, cut into squares and bake in moderate oven ten to fifteen minutes. Eat with cheese or butter.

Rich Plum Pudding.—To 1 lb. of flour stir in 2 teaspoonfuls of Sandow's Baking Powder, ½ teaspoonful of salt, 1 teaspoonful of allspice, and ¼ lb. of Jordan almonds blanched and minced, 6 ozs. mixed candied peel, chopped fine, 1 lb. of Demerara sugar, 1 lb. beef suet, shredded finely. Stone 1 lb. raisins and ½ lb. of prunes, wash and pick 1 lb. each currants and sultanas. When prepared chop separately the raisins, currants, sultanas and prunes. Stir these well into the mixture. Warm very slightly 1 lb. of golden syrup, add to it either ½ glass of ale or 1 egg. Stir into mixture thoroughly, and leave standing all night. Stir next morning. Put into buttered basins, tie down with floured cloths, and boil 7 hours.

Sandow Ideal Cake.—Make the cake from the following ingredients: 11 ounces of flour, 9 ounces of sugar, 6 ounces of butter, 1½ ounces Sandow's Vanillin sugar, or to taste, ½ pound sultanas, 1 new laid egg, 1 teaspoonful Sandow's H. F. Baking Powder. The above ingredients make a cake approximately 2½ pounds.

Pastry for Mince Pie.—To 1 lb. of flour add a dessertspoonful of castor sugar, a pinch of salt, and a teaspoonful of Sandow's H.F. Baking Powder. Knead in ½ lb. butter or lard. Add sufficient water or milk to make it into a fine paste. Roll well out on floured board. These ingredients should produce sufficient material for 18 to 20 mince pies.

Shortbread.—To 1 lb. flour add 1 lb. butter, 6 ozs. castor sugar and 1 teaspoonful Sandow's Baking Powder. Knead well and roll out on floured board to ½ inch thick. Add no moisture. Bake in moderate oven until a pale golden brown. These ingredients should produce two shortcakes about an inch thick.

IF YOU PREFER TO TRY BEFORE YOU BUY,

On receipt of your name and address, mentioning the offer in this paper, you will be sent a liberal free trial supply, together with a valuable illustrated cookery book, with over 100 special wholesome household recipes. Address:—Sandow's Health Foods, Ltd., Elephant and Castle, London, S.E.

"AFTER DINNER, THERE WOULD BE NO TV. FAMILIES WOULD ENJOY PARLOUR GAMES"

⊗ For Christmas dinner, goose was at this time still more common than turkey. The bird would be stuffed with chestnuts, pork and apple stuffing and sprinkled with fat and salt, then served with apple, gooseberry and bread sauces instead of cranberry.

Other delicacies on the Edwardian table included boar's head and sheep's tongues. After dinner, there would be no TV or computer games. Instead, families would enjoy parlour games such as Charades, and carols would be sung around the piano. ⊗

Above: From left, Glenn Nason, Una Stubbs, Harry Fowler and Amanda Barrie, watched by compere Ronan O'Casey, as they rehearse for the charades-based game show Don't Say A Word in 1963

THE ABBREVIATION XMAS ISN'T IRRELIGIOUS. THE LETTER X IS A GREEK ABBREVIATION FOR CHRIST.

⊘ The first specially-made festive films started to appear, with an adaptation of Charles Dickens' A Christmas Carol released in 1910.

The outbreak of the First World War in 1914 obviously had a serious impact on how families were able to celebrate Christmas. Men serving on the front line were unable to enjoy the occasion with their loved ones, and hundreds of thousands would never make it back.

There were also food shortages, with rationing later introduced for bread, tea, sugar and meat. Four years had passed by the time the conflict ended, with families finally able to look forward to a better future.

The front page of the Daily Mirror on Christmas Eve, 1918, read: "Everyone seems determined to celebrate the first Christmas of peace time in a manner that will make up for the grey Christmases of the war years.

"The festival of peace and goodwill can once again be held without any feeling that is a mockery, and family reunions can take place again without the ever-present fear of coming loss."

Above: A scene from A Christmas Carol in 1910

The Daily Mirror

WHY DELAY?

AN HISTORIC GROUP: BRITISH AND GERMAN SOLDIERS PHOTOGRAPHED TOGETHER.

CHRISTMAS TRUCE

JUST hours earlier both sides were desperately trying to kill each other.

But for a brief period over Christmas 1914, the bullets, bombs and bloodshed on the Western Front in the Great War gave way to a precious moment of festive peace.

All along the front line, battle-weary British and German soldiers laid down their guns and for a few hours at least – in some cases days – enjoyed some Christmas cheer.

"Just think," wrote one soldier to his family, "while you were eating turkey I was talking and shaking hands with the very men I had been trying to kill a few hours before!

"It was astounding!"

The Christmas truce of 1914 has come to represent a glimmer of humanity at the core of one of the deadliest conflicts which

saw 16 million die in four years. It began when German soldiers started to sing Christmas carols. British troops responded and gradually both sets of soldiers moved out of their trenches and met in no-man's land.

After exchanging stories and gifts, several games of football broke out.

The only result recorded was a 3-2 victory by the Germans, quoted in soldiers' letters from both sides.

British soldiers even wrote of cutting the hair of Germans, while others exchanged the buttons from their military jackets.

One young soldier wrote home: "They finished their carol and we thought that we ought to retaliate in some way, so we sang The First Noël,

and when we finished that they all began clapping; and then they struck up another favourite of theirs, O Tannenbaum."

On some parts of the front hostilities were officially resumed on Boxing Day at 8.30am – ceremonial pistol shots marking the occasion.

The story was at first restricted from being published but had come out by early 1915, and the Daily Mirror front page of January 5 shows a photo of mingling troops on the front.

1920-1939

LIFE GETS SWEETER AS WIRELESS GIFTS SIGNAL A TIME OF BIG CHANGES

A boom in chocolate production helped satisfy the nation's increasingly sweet tooth over the festive period, board games expanded massively and radio listeners heard King George V's first Christmas Day message.

Main picture: Betty Graves and her little brother Keith are pictured hanging up Christmas decorations in 1933. Top left, Coventry Council House adorned in decorations in 1935

CHRISTMAS dinner began to move decisively towards the turkey following the end of the First World War.

Buying a big bird was thought good value, although chicken or capons were far more common for poorer families. At the top end of society, goose, beef and other game birds were often still part of the Christmas menu, while a desire for sweet things and mass-manufactured chocolate bars by companies such as Cadbury were more prevalent by the 1930s.

Tinsel and cheap, pressed-metal decorations were now far more common, and electric fairy lights were also just starting to make their first appearances.

Board games expanded massively and were often aimed at children and adults, helping to bring the family together on Christmas Day.

Monopoly appeared in the mid-30s and other games around that time included L'Attaque – an early predecessor of Stretego – and Stumpz, which was based on a game of cricket. ⊘

Above: The Duchess of York – later the Queen Mother – helps with the preparation of a Christmas pudding at Market Harborough in 1927

Right: Evacuated children enjoy a Christmas meal at a hotel in Keswick, Cumbria, in 1939

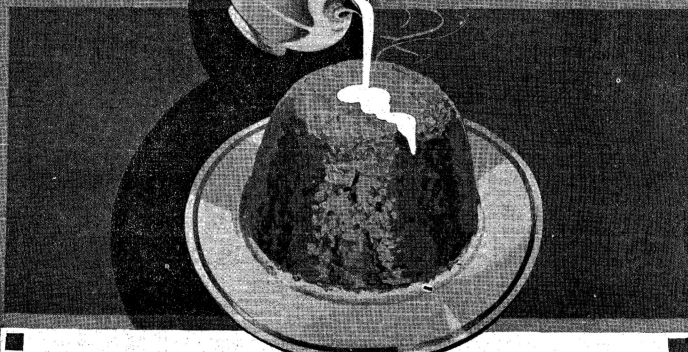

... and now the *gift* for thirst

Drink Coca-Cola
REG. U.S. PAT. OFF.

COPYRIGHT 1952, THE COCA-COLA COMPANY

⊘ The special Beano and Dandy annuals which were produced each year also became sought-after items.

The birth of the BBC in 1922 helped lead to the wireless becoming a popular Christmas present and special programmes would be broadcast over the festive period. Ten years later, King George V made his first Christmas broadcast, and listening to the King's Christmas Day speech became a habit across the Empire. Meanwhile, the modern portrayal of the red-and-white-robed Santa is often traced back to the 1930s Coca-Cola adverts, although the drinks company was simply following an image that had already been strongly established. ⊘

Above: An old Coca-Cola advert showing the modern-day image of Santa

"THOSE IN STEADY, STABLE EMPLOYMENT COULD AFFORD TO INDULGE A LITTLE"

⊙ Britain was affected by severe economic problems in the 1930s but low interest rates throughout the decade meant that those in steady, stable employment could afford to indulge a little.

But just as the horrors of the First World War were becoming a distant memory, by the end of the 1930s Europe had descended into conflict yet again.

Above: Caravan enthusiasts enjoy Christmas dinner in 1934

Right: Children at a Christmas party organised by the Royal British Legion in 1929

1940s

CHRISTMAS SPIRIT IS OUT IN FORCE DURING OUR DARKEST HOUR

With the outbreak of war and the introduction of rationing, families were forced to put many Christmas traditions on hold. However, people still did what they could to celebrate.

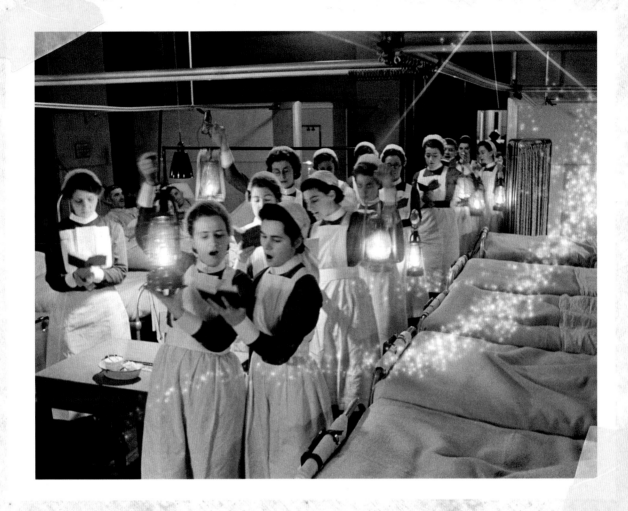

During the Blitz, many families spent some of the festive period in air-raid shelters and decked them out with makeshift decorations, with very short Christmas trees much in demand.

Magazines provided ideas for making decorations, such as lanterns from scraps of wallpaper.

Strips of metal foil called chaff – dropped by Nazis planes to confuse the radar into thinking there was a military attack – were also used as decoration.

As turkey was unaffordable, one alternative for Christmas dinner was cooking home-reared chickens or rabbits – with home-grown vegetables and chutneys also making it on the table.

Housewives had to create Christmas cakes and pudding without dried fruit or marzipan, instead using sponge or other unlikely ingredients, with alcohol being prohibitively expensive.

People were also discouraged from giving presents and urged to give as much as they could to the war effort. Almost £10 million in war bonds was sold in the week before Christmas 1940. ⊙

Above: A scene at Westminster Hospital on Christmas Eve in 1940

Right: A family inside an air-raid shelter during the Second World War

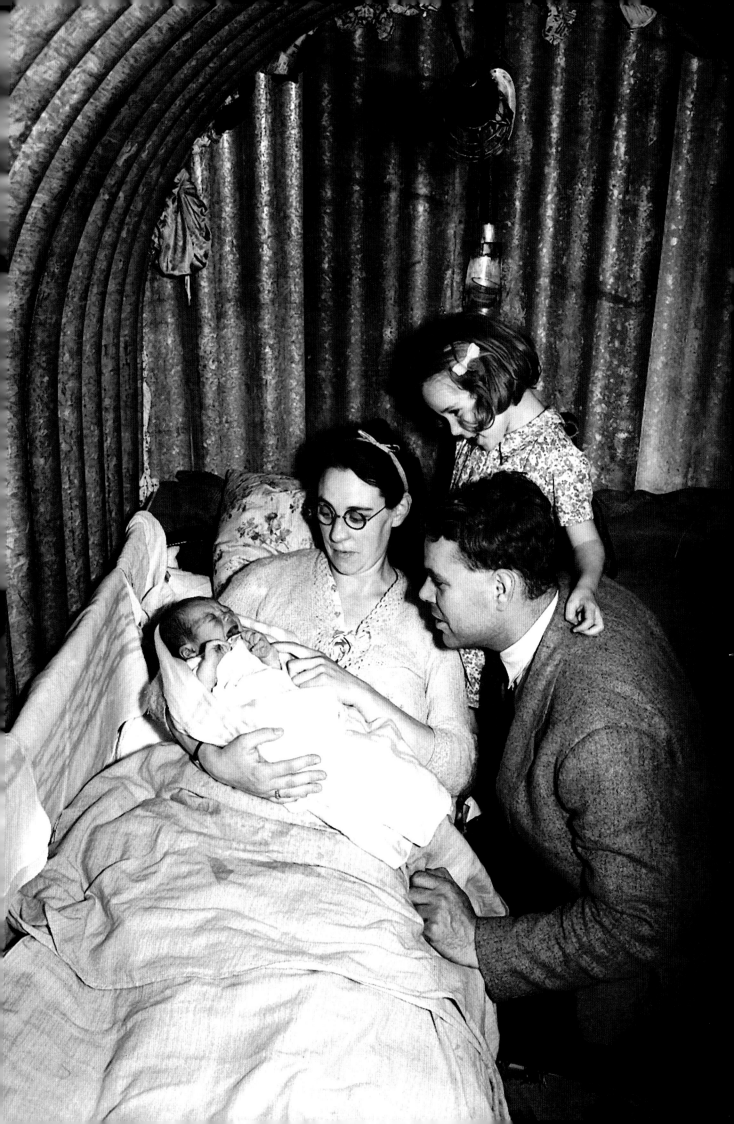

"THE WOMEN'S VOLUNTARY SERVICES TOOK ON THE TASK OF LIFTING SPIRITS DURING THE CONFLICT"

Above: WVS volunteers serve tea and sandwiches to people in an underground air-raid shelter

As the war continued, people were increasingly given air-raid-shelter-friendly presents, with flasks, sleeping bags and even 'gas masks' for dolls proving popular.

The Women's Voluntary Services (WVS) took on the task of lifting spirits during the conflict, distributing warm clothing and blankets to families who had lost everything, and organising dances for adults and parties for children.

To try to recreate some of the festive magic, the volunteers encouraged people to make Christmas gifts for children, showing how toy trains could be created out of ordinary pieces of wood and doll houses made from household waste such as matchboxes.

Above: An Army officer plays with a toy train set with children from a Barnardo's care home in 1944

Below: German prisoners of war with toys they made for the children of dead and injured British servicemen

DID YOU KNOW?

THE LONG SHOPPING SPREE BEFORE CHRISTMAS BEGAN IN AMERICA WHEN RELATIVES OF SOLDIERS POSTED OVERSEAS IN THE SECOND WORLD WAR WERE ENCOURAGED TO MAIL GIFTS EARLY.

Top: A family hanging up Christmas decorations in 1944

Above: A woman with a bunch of twigs and branches to decorate her home at Christmas

Right: Soldier Stanley Kerr decorates his little Christmas tree while on war duty in Holland

> "THE RELEASE OF CLASSIC FILMS 'IT'S A WONDERFUL LIFE' AND 'MIRACLE ON 34TH STREET' IN THE SECOND HALF OF THE DECADE HELPED PROVIDE SOME LIGHT FESTIVE RELIEF"

⊘ The end of the war in 1945 did not mean an end to austerity and some form of rationing would remain in place until 1954, when restrictions on the sale of meat and bacon were lifted.

However, the release of classic films It's A Wonderful Life and Miracle On 34th Street in the second half of the decade helped provide some light festive relief, while new games such as Cluedo and Scrabble would prove popular Christmas presents for decades to come.

Left: Edmund Gwenn, Natalie Wood and Maureen O'Hara in a scene from the 1947 film Miracle On 34th Street

DID YOU KNOW?

THE WORD CHRISTMAS COMES FROM THE OLD ENGLISH "CRISTES MAESSE" MEANING "CHRIST'S MASS".

1950s

QUEEN'S SPEECH AND THE HIGH NOTES OF FEEL-GOOD FIFTIES

The post-war austerity years put a break on the growing commercialisation of Christmas but it wasn't long before the spending spree started again – and we could sing along to the very first festive chart-topper.

Main picture: The son of film director Richard Attenborough, Michael, is seen here enchanted by the family Christmas tree in December 1952

Rationing measures may still have been in place until the middle of the decade but, by 1957, the British public had "never had it so good", prime minister Harold Macmillan famously said.

Full employment combined with an unprecedented rise in consumerism meant millions of Britons saw their standard of living rise – and the Christmas spending spree recommenced.

It was a decade in which the first UK music chart was published – and so began the pop culture phenomenon of the Christmas number one single, first secured by Al Martino in 1952 with his song Here In My Heart. ⊙

Top: A family open their presents next to the Christmas tree in 1959

Above: A customer is handed a pack of butter in May 1954 after rationing restrictions are lifted

Right: Peggy Waters was on hand to do people's Christmas shopping – for seven shillings and six pence an hour – in December 1953

"JUST IMAGINE YOU ARE TALKING TO ONE VIEWER — PRINCE PHILIP"

⊘ That year, Britain's new monarch, Queen Elizabeth II, delivered her first festive message to the nation, followed five years later by her maiden Christmas Day television speech.

The Daily Mirror reported how the young Queen was told by her advisers to think of the appearance as "an intimate fireside talk" and "just imagine you are talking to one viewer – Prince Philip". ⊘

Left: Windmill Girls Rosemary Phillips and Kathleen Cooper putting up Christmas decorations in their dressing room at the Windmill Theatre in London in 1953

Above: A family watching the Queen's first televised festive message in 1957

> **"THE BIRTH OF ITV IN 1955 OPENED ANOTHER DOOR TO ADVERTISERS WANTING TO REACH CONSUMERS IN THE RUN-UP TO CHRISTMAS"**

Top: The hula-hooping craze had caught on at St Paul's Way Secondary Central School in Bow, London, in September 1958

Above right: Women and children looking through Selfridges' shop window on Oxford Street, London, the week before Christmas in 1955

CHRISTMAS NUMBER 1s

1952 AL MARTINO
"HERE IN MY HEART"

1953 FRANKIE LAINE
"ANSWER ME"

1954 WINIFRED ATWELL
"LET'S HAVE ANOTHER PARTY"

1955 DICKIE VALENTINE
"CHRISTMAS ALPHABET"

1956 JOHNNIE RAY
"JUST WALKIN' IN THE RAIN"

1957 HARRY BELAFONTE
"MARY'S BOY CHILD"

1958 CONWAY TWITTY
"IT'S ONLY MAKE BELIEVE"

1959 EMILE FORD & THE
CHECKMATES "WHAT DO YOU WANT
TO MAKE THOSE EYES AT ME FOR?"

DID YOU KNOW?

THE WORLD'S TALLEST
CHRISTMAS TREE, AT 221FT
HIGH, WAS ERECTED IN
WASHINGTON IN 1950.

> There was a big growth in the number of people owning television sets and the birth of ITV in 1955 opened another door to advertisers wanting to reach consumers in the run-up to Christmas.

Among the best-known toys of the decade was the Hula-Hoop, while the Frisbee and Play-Doh were also popular gifts for children.

And in the days before broadcasters created festive editions of virtually all their most popular shows, there was a Christmas special of The Goon Show on the BBC Home Service in 1956, while the big movies of the decade included White Christmas, Frosty The Snowman and Scrooge. >

Above: The Goons, from left, Harry Secombe, Spike Milligan and Peter Sellers

One tradition which was coming to an end was the Christmas Day football match, largely due to a lack of public transport and the wish of fans to stay at home.

Christmas Day and Boxing Day double-headers were a routine part of the fixture list until 1957, after which time they fell out of favour, and topsy-turvy results could be expected.

Derby County, for instance, responded to their 4-1 thumping at Everton on Christmas Day in 1946 by thrashing the same opponents 5-1 just 24 hours later.

The final December 25 game took place between Blackpool and Blackburn Rovers in 1965.

Above: Arsenal v Chelsea at a snow-covered Highbury Stadium on Boxing Day in 1956

Right: Bristol Rovers score against Swansea Town in their Division Two match on December 26, 1957

"ONE TRADITION WHICH WAS COMING TO AN END WAS THE CHRISTMAS DAY FOOTBALL MATCH"

Daily Mirror Teleguide

TELLY CHRISTMAS!

with £50,000 of star talent

TELEVISION'S three-day Christmas schedule offers viewers the biggest talent line-up of the year.

Few of TV's top stars will be missing from the screens of ITV and B.B.C. viewers. The bill for talent alone will top £50,000 on both channels.

And since last year the standard of recording TV programmes in advance has improved 100 per cent. —thanks to a new method of filming on magnetic tape.

This system has been used extensively—with the result that most of the shows are already "in the can."

Viewers will be unable to spot any difference in quality between these recorded Christmas programmes and normal live shows.

And the recording method will enable many performers working in pantomime to appear also on TV over Christmas.

Other performers can spend the holiday away from the TV studios— watching themselves on the screen.

This is how some of them will be spending the holiday. . . .

★ GRACIE FIELDS (A-Z Christmas Eve, B.B.C., 7.30 p.m.) will be in her Capri home with husband Boris—for the first time in the seven years they have been married.

Gracie reports by phone: "Boris and I will sit by the fire and listen to the Queen on the extra-powerful radio set he has made for us.

"We have sent the staff away and will be entirely on our own, although

● American singer Harry Belafonte. He plans a family Christmas Day at his new home in New York (see him on B.B.C. TV tomorrow).

I expect friends will drop in. Here we shall have all I want: peace and quiet."

★ HUGHIE GREEN ("Double Your Money," Christmas Day, ITV, 7.30 p.m.) will make his first-ever appearance in pantomime at Streatham Hill on Boxing Day. He plays in "Aladdin"—as Abanazar

● This three-day Teleguide has been prepared by CLIFFORD DAVIS, JACK BELL and RICHARD SEAR to help you see the best of the Christmas viewing

the "dirty old uncle." He says: "Anyone who calls this true-to-type casting will be crossed off my Christmas card list."

He will stop rehearsals on Christmas Day to watch himself on TV.

SEEING HIMSELF

★ DICK BENTLEY ("Alf's Button," Christmas Day, ITV, 8.0 p.m.) is spending Christmas with his wife, Peta, at their London home.

"Watch my own show? Of course," he says. "In one of the sequences I am surrounded by pretty girls—I only

hope my wife won't get the wrong idea."

★ PERRY COMO ("Christmas Night with the Stars," B.B.C., 6.25 p.m., and "The Perry Como Show," Boxing Day, B.B.C., 7.30 p.m.) will be up early to attend church in Long Island, New York.

Later in the morning Perry, his wife Roselle, their two sons and their daughter will exchange Christmas presents.

Perry is keeping his gifts secret—but they won't be lavish, for he doesn't believe in spoiling children.

After a turkey dinner Perry will help with the washing-up.

Most of the day he will spend lounging around in slacks and a pullover.

★ HARRY BELAFONTE (Christmas Day, B.B.C., 7.46 and 11.52 p.m.) and his family will spend the most exciting Christmas they have ever had.

Yesterday they moved into a ten-room flat on New York's West Side.

For months Harry has been trying to find a home, and he always came up against the brick wall of colour bar.

He and his wife Julie will spend tomorrow with their family.

★ ALFRED MARKS ("Life With The Lyons," Boxing Day, ITV, 6.10 p.m.) is getting a Father Christmas outfit for a "command performance" for his two children, Danielle, aged three and a half, and Gareth, nine weeks.

★ MICHAEL MEDWIN ("The Army Game," Boxing Day, ITV, 8.30 p.m.) is throwing a party in an oak-beamed cottage at Sunningdale, Berks.

"It will be champagne with cigars," he announces. Joining him will be Norman "Cupcake" Rossington, who will cook a full scale Christmas dinner for a dozen or more.

He reports: "I used to cook for eighty coppers in a police canteen—this will be easy."

● A yuletide kiss. Peggy Mount and David Kossoff in "Christmas The Larkins" (ITV, Boxing Day, 10.15 p.m.).

Above: This Daily Mirror article features the highlights from the Christmas television schedule of 1958, when improving technology meant more shows could be recorded in advance, enabling the stars to spend the festive period at home rather than in the studio

DECEMBER 24, 1954:

Six thousand Army and RAF men were told their Christmas leave had been cancelled due to the threat of flooding.

Many of them were called back to their barracks in North and East England as they waited on station platforms for homeward-bound trains. The servicemen were told to stand by for flood duties as 80mph gales lashed Britain. As the night fell and the weather conditions improved, 4,000 men were told they could go home as planned.

DECEMBER 24, 1955:

Carol singers performing in front of the Royal Family made a last-minute change to their set – at the request of Prince Charles.

Silent Night – a favourite with the young prince – was originally missing from the list of carols to be sung at Sandringham House.

The singers duly obliged with Charles' special request and the seven-year-old "joined in lustily" as he sat up to watch the performance with his parents.

ALBERT Asch feared the worst after his beloved dog Sally fell ill shortly before Christmas in 1957.

Surgeons thought the 14-year-old mongrel, who had been taken to the PDSA veterinary hospital in Ilford, was too old to survive an operation.

During surgery, Ms Asch composed a poem as a prayer for his dog, and Sally made it through.

On Christmas Eve, as can be seen above, she was back at the fireside, settled down with her head snuggled on Mr Asch's slippery feet.

Speaking at his home in Chiswick, Mr Asch said: "The miracle has happened. The return of Sally is the most wonderful Christmas present I've ever had."

" SALLY IS THE MOST WONDERFUL CHRISTMAS PRESENT I'VE EVER HAD "

1960s

ACTION **man** SOLDIER *by palitoy*

NOW WITH GRIPPING HANDS

TOY HEAVEN AND BEATLES MANIA IN THE SUPER SIXTIES

Children could enjoy a wider range of toys than ever before and wives were 'treated' to the latest labour-saving devices during a decade in which commercial television helped encourage a longer festive shopping period.

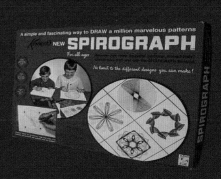

A simple and fascinating way to DRAW a million marvelous patterns

NEW **SPIROGRAPH**

For all ages

No limit to the different designs you can make!

Main picture: Three-year-old David Smith enjoys driving his new go-kart in 1969

HOB 1

Following a decade in which Britain had turned into a mass consumerist society, children growing up in the 1960s could expect a greater range of toys for Christmas.

Typical gifts for boys included Scalextric racing car sets and Thunderbird toys, while girls could expect costumes, Sindy dolls and play kitchens.

Teenagers were more likely to receive transistor radios, as well as a wide range of popular music annuals and guides.

Spacehoppers, introduced in 1969, would go on to become a major craze for youngsters of all ages. ⊘

Top: Children look longingly at toys through a shop window in December 1960

Right: Young Susan Burton talks to a policeman while holding a pile of Christmas presents in 1961

"MORE PEOPLE WERE DRINKING WINE, AT LEAST PARTLY DUE TO THE GROWTH IN SUPERMARKETS"

Left: Christmas shoppers inside Coventry's City Arcade shopping precinct in 1962

Above: Two women pour themselves a drink at a Christmas party in 1969

Right: Crowds turn out to see a Christmas tree illuminated in Trafalgar Square in 1961

❯ Cigarette lighters and electric razors were among the gifts often given to men, who would be encouraged to "treat" their wives to labour-saving devices such as vacuum cleaners and washing machines.

More people were drinking wine by this period, at least partly due to the growth in supermarkets, where increasing numbers of people were buying vegetables to go with their turkey. ❯

Above: Father Christmas helps seven-year-old Susan Stevens, of Castle Bromwich, pull a cracker at a party held in Birmingham in 1960

Above right: A turkey auction at Smithfield Poultry Market, London, in 1961

Top right: Children from Foleshill Day Nursery in Coventry perform a nativity play in December 1964

Far right: Some of the electrical domestic appliances which were available in the 1960s

" WIVES WERE 'TREATED' TO LABOUR-SAVING DEVICES "

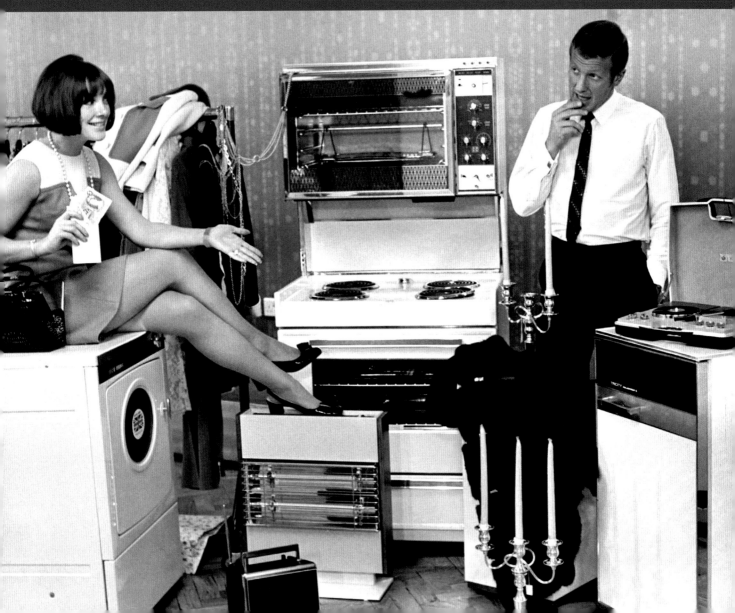

Top: A night view of the Christmas lights in Regent Street, London, in 1965

Above: People shopping for Christmas presents at a London market in 1960

" COMMERCIAL TELEVISION DID MUCH TO ENCOURAGE A PROLONGED FESTIVE SHOPPING PERIOD "

CHRISTMAS MOVIES

> Commercial television did much to encourage a prolonged festive shopping period and Christmas trees – which began to go up earlier than in previous decades – started to be decorated with cheap, plastic ornaments and fairy lights. With post-war immigration to countries like Australia and Canada spreading families wider, the sending of Christmas cards and messages also became more popular.

It was a decade that also saw the first Morecambe and Wise Christmas special, with festive editions of Dr Who, Till Death Us Do Part, Not Only... But Also, Thunderbirds, Stingray and The Avengers also being broadcast. Fans of The Beatles helped propel the band to the top of the festive music charts on four occasions during this period, with Elvis Presley, Tom Jones and Cliff Richards & The Shadows also hitting the top spot.

DR. SEUSS' HOW THE GRINCH STOLE CHRISTMAS

SANTA CLAUS CONQUERS THE MARTIANS

BABES IN TOYLAND

MAGIC CHRISTMAS TREE

SANTA'S CHRISTMAS CIRCUS

CHRISTMAS THAT ALMOST WASN'T

SCROOGE MCDUCK AND MONEY

A CHRISTMAS FANTASY

HEIDI

CHRISTMAS ON EARTH

CHRISTMAS NUMBER 1s

1960 CLIFF RICHARD & THE SHADOWS
"I LOVE YOU"

1961 DANNY WILLIAMS
"MOON RIVER"

1962 ELVIS PRESLEY
"RETURN TO SENDER"

1963 THE BEATLES
"I WANT TO HOLD YOUR HAND"

1964 THE BEATLES
"I FEEL FINE"

1965 THE BEATLES
"DAY TRIPPER" / "WE CAN WORK IT OUT"

1966 TOM JONES
"GREEN, GREEN GRASS OF HOME"

1967 THE BEATLES
"HELLO, GOODBYE"

1968 THE SCAFFOLD
"LILY THE PINK"

1969 ROLF HARRIS
"TWO LITTLE BOYS"

DID YOU KNOW?

JINGLE BELLS WAS THE FIRST SONG BROADCAST FROM SPACE WHEN GEMINI 6 ASTRONAUTS TOM STAFFORD AND WALLY SCHIRRA SANG IT ON DECEMBER 16, 1965.

NEWSFLASH

DECEMBER 24, 1968:

Spectacular photographs of the Earth from deep space were captured for the first time. They were taken aboard Apollo 8, whose crew – Frank Borman, Jim Lovell and Bill Anders – were the first people to orbit the Moon, flying around the far side which is not visible from Earth.

> Meanwhile, electrical shavers from German-based Braun and Dutch company Philips also proved popular gifts, as Britain's entry into the European Common Market lowered the cost of importing goods from abroad.

The first video games console also entered the market in the 1970s, while consumers kept a close eye on the latest gadgets coming out of Japan, such as the portable cassette player. >

Left: Christmas shoppers on Northumberland Street, in Newcastle, in December 1971

Above: The Beatles and, left, the huge queue for tickets to see the band's Christmas concert in Liverpool in 1963

DECEMBER 24, 1969:

It looked like being a bleak Christmas for pensioner Albert Hebbes and his wife Nora after a conman swindled them out of their savings.

A bogus council official had turned up at the couple's home in Slough and said the roof needed retiling.

After 75-year-old Nora handed over an £11 downpayment, the man went away and never came back.

The crime touched the hearts of the local police and, after a whip-round among the officers, they handed over £20 to the couple.

The landlord of Albert's local pub also turned up with a turkey and bottles of Christmas cheer after organising a separate collection.

Nora said: "Everyone has been so kind. Now I'm going to get Albert a present."

> " EVERYONE HAS BEEN SO KIND. NOW I'M GOING TO GET ALBERT A PRESENT "

1970s

A SACKFUL OF LAUGHS AS WE SIT DOWN TO WATCH COMEDY CLASSICS

A grim decade? Actually, the 1970s was a time when families really started splashing the cash over the festive period, while the Morecambe and Wise Christmas special became an institution

Main picture: Eric Morecambe and Ernie Wise with actress Kate O'Mara, who appeared in the comedy duo's 1976 Christmas special. Top left, a scene from Steptoe And Son

It is remembered as a time of economic strife – but the 1970s was also a decade when families really started splashing out at Christmas.

This was partly due to the growing sophistication of advertising, as companies became more adept at identifying their target audience.

Children would hassle their parents for the latest Action Man toy or Barbie doll they had seen on television.

Husbands were encouraged to show further consideration for their wives by buying them labour-saving devices such as electric carving knives, while Quality Street would be promoted as a chocolate treat for all the family.

Grooming products were also being aimed at men for the first time, with Brut commercials featuring the likes of boxing legend Henry Cooper and football star Kevin Keegan helping to change the perception that scents were only for women. ⊙

Above: The children of staff at Birmingham car dealers Prestage Ltd enjoy a Christmas party in 1973

Right: A young boy is pictured surrounded by toys in 1970

Meanwhile, electrical shavers from German-based Braun and Dutch company Philips also proved popular gifts, as Britain's entry into the European Common Market lowered the cost of importing goods from abroad.

The first video games console also entered the market in the 1970s, while consumers kept a close eye on the latest gadgets coming out of Japan, such as the portable cassette player. ⊙

Left: Christmas shoppers on Northumberland Street, in Newcastle, in December 1971

CHRISTMAS MOVIES

THE STORY OF CHRISTMAS

THE BEAR'S CHRISTMAS

CHRISTMAS MORNING

TUKIKI AND HIS SEARCH FOR A MERRY CHRISTMAS

A CHRISTMAS CAROL

HEIDI

SHEILA'S CHRISTMAS

CHRISTMAS SNOWS, CHRISTMAS WINDS

CHRISTMAS AT MOOSE FACTORY

DID YOU KNOW?

SCIENTISTS HAVE CALCULATED THAT SANTA WOULD HAVE TO VISIT 822 HOMES A SECOND TO DELIVER ALL THE WORLD'S PRESENTS ON CHRISTMAS EVE, TRAVELLING AT 650 MILES A SECOND.

"THE BBC STEPPED UP ITS EFFORTS OVER THE CHRISTMAS PERIOD"

⊗ By now virtually every household had a television and the BBC stepped up its efforts over the Christmas period, with regular festive editions of Are You Being Served?, Dad's Army and, of course, the unforgettable Morecambe and Wise.

Eddie Braben, the writer behind the comedy duo, once said people judged the quality of their Christmas on the quality of the Morecambe and Wise Christmas Special. It was also the decade that saw the release of the Slade classic Merry Xmas Everybody, with Queen's Bohemian Rhapsody and Wings' Mull Of Kintyre also hitting the festive number one spot.

Main picture: Carry On stars Sid James and Barbara Windsor were among the entertainers who gathered to promote ITV's Christmas schedule in 1973

Left and above: Radio One disc jockey Noel Edmonds, dressed as Father Christmas, and the cast of Are Your Being Served?

CHRISTMAS SPECIALS

Above: The cast of Coronation Street celebrate Christmas at the Rovers Return in 1974

DID YOU KNOW?

THE LARGEST CHRISTMAS CRACKER, 45.72M LONG AND 3.04M IN DIAMETER, WAS PULLED IN AUSTRALIA IN 1991.

DECEMBER 23, 1970:

Little Samantha Greenwood tried something a little seasonal for breakfast – a generous helping of berries off the Christmas holly.

The two-year-old was taken to hospital after telling her horrified mother: "I've been eating these sweeties."

Holly berries are poisonous to humans and eating them can cause drowsiness, vomiting and dehydration.

Fortunately, Samantha suffered no serious effects and was back at her Leeds home in plenty of time for Christmas.

1970 DAVE EDMUNDS
"I HEAR YOU KNOCKING"

1971 BENNY HILL
"ERNIE (THE FASTEST MILKMAN IN THE WEST)"

1972 JIMMY OSMOND
"LONG HAIRED LOVER FROM LIVERPOOL"

1973 SLADE
"MERRY XMAS EVERYBODY"

1974 MUD
"LONELY THIS CHRISTMAS"

1975 QUEEN
"BOHEMIAN RHAPSODY"

1976 JOHNNY MATHIS
"WHEN A CHILD IS BORN (SOLEADO)"

1977 WINGS
"MULL OF KINTYRE" / "GIRLS' SCHOOL"

1978 BONEY M.
"MARY'S BOY CHILD — OH MY LORD"

1979 PINK FLOYD
"ANOTHER BRICK IN THE WALL (PART 2)"

NEWSFLASH

DECEMBER 24, 1974:

An army of 150 white-bearded Santas were arrested by police – after handing out stolen gifts in the streets.

They had loaded their sacks by stripping the counters at top stores without paying, and handed out the goodies to children in Copenhagen, Denmark, as part of a protest against the commercialism of Christmas.

Right: How the Daily Mirror reported the story in 1974

Christmas Mirror

EUROPE'S BIGGEST DAILY SALE

5p Tuesday, December 24, 1974 No. 22,060

SANTA, YOU'RE UNDER ARREST

1980s

BIG-SPENDING SHOPPERS ADD MORE SPARKLE TO THE FESTIVE MAGIC

A 'festival of awesome over-indulgence' it may have been but Christmas in the 1980s was also a time when families came together in their millions to watch classic comedies and blockbuster movies, while a certain song urged us all to help 'feed the world'.

Main picture: As the snow came down in December 1981, workers at a coach company in London cheered themselves up by creating a 15ft snowman

A "festival of awesome over-indulgence and spending" is how one historian has described Christmas in the 1980s.

It was the decade when the earlier start to the festive season became even more apparent, with many cities putting up their decorations in November in an attempt to lure shoppers.

This encouraged families to follow suit, and the expansion of the electronics industry meant exterior decorative lighting was beginning to add a new element to domestic Christmas traditions.

Another change could be seen on the dinner table as desserts offered by supermarkets – such as Wall's Viennetta – started competing with the Christmas pudding. ⊘

Above: Confectioner Angela Marcanto tucks into a Christmas pudding ice cream in 1986

Right: A giant Christmas tree on display at Manchester's Arndale Centre in 1987

"A WIDER RANGE OF ELECTRONIC PRODUCTS CAME ON THE MARKET"

❯ A wider range of electronic products came on the market, and popular presents included the latest computer consoles from Nintendo and Sega and the first portable CD players, along with BMX bikes, Transformers, Care Bears, Cabbage Patch Kids and My Little Pony.

The introduction of Camcorders, meanwhile, enabled families to record their Christmas memories and watch them over and over again. ❯

Above: Father Christmas giving Rudolf the Reindeer a ride in 1980

Top left: Four-year-old Laura Tyrell points Father Christmas in the right direction after he gets lost looking for Greenland

Left: Santa on his sleigh in the snow in December 1981

> While parents could take the children to the cinema to watch films such as Santa Claus: The Movie, Scrooged and National Lampoon's Christmas Vacation, television companies were also paying large sums for the rights to blockbuster movies – such as Indiana Jones And The Temple Of Doom – and the small screen was also giving old film classics a new lease of life.

The video recorder gave people the option to watch programmes at their leisure and, with most families now owning more than one television set, children could go off and watch separate things from their parents.

But the television still brought families together and huge numbers would watch shows aired on Christmas Day – such as the 30 million people who tuned in to EastEnders to see Den Watts hand divorce papers to wife Angie in 1986.

Festive editions of Only Fools And Horses become an almost annual event in the 1980s, while the Christmas specials of The Two Ronnies were also big hits. >

Main picture: The stars of ITV's Christmas season, including Eric Morecambe, Jill Gascoine and Gordon Jackson

Above right: Comedian Ronnie Corbett turns on Newcastle's Christmas lights in 1989

Right: EastEnders characters Den and Angie Watts, played by Leslie Grantham and Anita Dobson

CHRISTMAS MOVIES

A CHRISTMAS STORY

CHRISTMAS VACATION

COMFORT AND JOY

SCROOGED

DON'T OPEN 'TILL CHRISTMAS

ONE MAGIC CHRISTMAS

PRANCER

SANTA CLAUS: THE MOVIE

ERNEST SAVES CHRISTMAS

MICKEY'S CHRISTMAS CAROL

" TELEVISION COMPANIES WERE PAYING LARGE SUMS FOR THE RIGHTS TO BLOCKBUSTER MOVIES "

CHRISTMAS NUMBER 1s

1980 ST WINIFRED'S SCHOOL CHOIR
"THERE'S NO ONE QUITE LIKE GRANDMA"

1981 THE HUMAN LEAGUE
"DON'T YOU WANT ME"

1982 RENÉE AND RENATO
"SAVE YOUR LOVE"

1983 THE FLYING PICKETS
"ONLY YOU"

1984 BAND AID
"DO THEY KNOW IT'S CHRISTMAS?"

1985 SHAKIN' STEVENS
"MERRY CHRISTMAS EVERYONE"

1986 JACKIE WILSON
"REET PETITE"

1987 PET SHOP BOYS
"ALWAYS ON MY MIND"

1988 CLIFF RICHARD
"MISTLETOE AND WINE"

1989 BAND AID II
"DO THEY KNOW IT'S CHRISTMAS?"

CHRISTMAS SPECIALS

TERRY AND JUNE (1980)

MINDER (1983)

ONLY FOOLS AND HORSES (1981-83 AND 1985-89)

JUST GOOD FRIENDS (1984)

THE TWO OF US (1988)

'ALLO 'ALLO! (1985)

BREAD (1988, 1989)

BLACKADDER (1988)

IN SICKNESS AND IN HEALTH (1989)

BRITAIN'S BEST-SELLING FESTIVE SINGLE IS BAND AID'S 1984 TRACK, DO THEY KNOW IT'S CHRISTMAS?, WHICH SOLD 3.5 MILLION COPIES.

⊙ Cliff Richard enjoyed his first solo Christmas number one single with Mistletoe and Wine in 1988, although the decade's most memorable song was Band Aid's charity classic Do They Know It's Christmas? which topped the charts twice, in 1984 and 1989.

Above: Terry and June – played by Terry Scott and June Whitfield – pull a cracker in a scene from the Christmas edition of the show in 1980

" FESTIVE EDITIONS OF ONLY FOOLS AND HORSES BECAME AN ALMOST ANNUAL EVENT "

After all the cuts and   tragedies, an NHS story that's really good news

SON'S THREE SILENT YEARS

MY MIRACLE

CHRISTMAS Mirror

Join the stars in your super SPARKLING XMAS MIRROR

Thursday, December 24, 1987   FORWARD WITH BRITAIN   20p

Your full **tv** Holiday GUIDE

IT'S A CRACKER!

The miracle of Edwin, and a smile that says it for all of us

HAPPY XMAS

I can talk at last

By JILL PALMER

Picture: ARTHUR SIDEY

MY MIRACLE PAGES 4 & 5

MY WORD! Excited Edwin looks forward to his first talking Christmas with his mum Victoria.

JOYFUL: Dad Jamie

By Jill Palmer

Pictures by Arthur Sidey

Plucky Edwin talks at last

CHRISTMAS CRACKER: Sparkling-eyed Edwin has so much to talk about.

'Now every single   word he says is wonderful to us'

Toddler Edwin Borwick had much to talk about while celebrating Christmas – after being given the gift of speech.

The three-year-old was born with such complex heart defects that doctors feared it would be impossible to operate.

His heart had to be completely rebuilt as Edwin underwent 15 operations in his first year.

The youngster pulled through and, after years of silence, the last hurdle was a throat operation to remove a breathing aid inserted after his windpipe collapsed.

In 1987, as Edwin noisily played with his Christmas games and sang along with nursery rhymes, parents Victoria and Jamie could not have been happier.

His mother said: "This is the time we have waited and longed for. It has been a long fight but Edwin has come through it. He is only using baby talk, saying odd words.

"But to us everything he says is wonderful."